Cut

by Crystal Skillman

A Samuel French Acting Edition

SAMUELFRENCH.COM

Copyright © 2012 by Crystal Skillman

ALL RIGHTS RESERVED

Cover Artwork by BellBoy Creative
bellboycreative.com

CAUTION: Professionals and amateurs are hereby warned that *CUT* is subject to a licensing fee. It is fully protected under the copyright laws of the United States of America, the British Commonwealth, including Canada, and all other countries of the Copyright Union. All rights, including professional, amateur, motion picture, recitation, lecturing, public reading, radio broadcasting, television and the rights of translation into foreign languages are strictly reserved. In its present form the play is dedicated to the reading public only.

The amateur and professional live stage performance rights to *CUT* are controlled exclusively by Samuel French, Inc., and licensing arrangements and performance licenses must be secured well in advance of presentation. PLEASE NOTE that amateur licensing fees are set upon application in accordance with your producing circumstances. When applying for a licensing quotation and a performance license please give us the number of performances intended, dates of production, your seating capacity and admission fee. Licensing fees are payable one week before the opening performance of the play to Samuel French, Inc., at 45 W. 25th Street, New York, NY 10010.

Licensing fee of the required amount must be paid whether the play is presented for charity or gain and whether or not admission is charged.

Professional/Stock licensing fees quoted upon application to Samuel French, Inc.

For all other rights than those stipulated above, apply to: The Gersh Agency, 41 Madison Avenue, 33rd Floor, New York, NY 10010.

Particular emphasis is laid on the question of amateur or professional readings, permission and terms for which must be secured in writing from Samuel French, Inc.

Copying from this book in whole or in part is strictly forbidden by law, and the right of performance is not transferable.

Whenever the play is produced the following notice must appear on all programs, printing and advertising for the play: "Produced by special arrangement with Samuel French, Inc."

Due authorship credit must be given on all programs, printing and advertising for the play.

ISBN 978-0-573-70012-5   Printed in U.S.A.   #20244

No one shall commit or authorize any act or omission by which the copyright of, or the right to copyright, this play may be impaired.

No one shall make any changes in this play for the purpose of production.

Publication of this play does not imply availability for performance. Both amateurs and professionals considering a production are strongly advised in their own interests to apply to Samuel French, Inc., for written permission before starting rehearsals, advertising, or booking a theatre.

No part of this book may be reproduced, stored in a retrieval system, or transmitted in any form, by any means, now known or yet to be invented, including mechanical, electronic, photocopying, recording, videotaping, or otherwise, without the prior written permission of the publisher.

MUSIC USE NOTE

Licensees are solely responsible for obtaining formal written permission from copyright owners to use copyrighted music in the performance of this play and are strongly cautioned to do so. If no such permission is obtained by the licensee, then the licensee must use only original music that the licensee owns and controls. Licensees are solely responsible and liable for all music clearances and shall indemnify the copyright owners of the play and their licensing agent, Samuel French, Inc., against any costs, expenses, losses and liabilities arising from the use of music by licensees.

IMPORTANT BILLING AND CREDIT REQUIREMENTS

All producers of *CUT must* give credit to the Author of the Play in all programs distributed in connection with performances of the Play, and in all instances in which the title of the Play appears for the purposes of advertising, publicizing or otherwise exploiting the Play and/or a production. The name of the Author *must* appear on a separate line on which no other name appears, immediately following the title and *must* appear in size of type not less than fifty percent of the size of the title type.

In addition the following credit must be given in all programs and publicity information distributed in association with this piece:

CUT was originally produced by
The Management in 2011,
New York City.

CUT was originally produced as a
ten-minute play presented by
Special Sauce Company.

CUT was first produced by Horse Trade and The Management in New York City on May 19, 2011. The performance was directed by Meg Sturiano, with sets by Kyle Dixon, costumes by Megan Hill, lighting by Grant Wilcoxen, and sound by Meg Sturiano and Joe Varca. The Production Stage Manager was Kelly Ruth Cole. The cast was as follows:

DANNO . . . . Joe Varca
COLETTE . . . . Megan Hill
RENE . . . . Nicole Beerman

Note: The full-length version of *CUT* was commissioned/developed with The Management (based on a ten-minute version presented by Special Sauce Company).

CUT received its Boston premiere on March 23, 2012 at Apollinaire Theatre Company (Danielle Fauteux Jacques, Artistic Director). It was directed by A. Vincent Ularich, with Paul "Beatle" Ring as the Stage Manager, and Erica Paige Brown as the Production Stage Manager. The cast was as follows:

DANNO . . . . Stewart Evan Smith
COLETTE . . . . Alyce Householter
RENE . . . . Elizabeth Anne Rimar

CHARACTERS

DANNO – Editor. 29
COLETTE – Logger. 26
RENE – Planner. 31
All three are reality TV show writers.

TIME

Now, Spring.

SETTING AND NOTES

A production office in LA. A working room of reality TV show writers.

At some points they speak as if to the audience/or camera in their head (each "I believe" moment operates like the talking head interviews in reality TV shows for instance).

Whenever they do speak in the scenes where they're in a race to finish, they're very much in the middle of the activity they describe (cutting, logging, story planning, running down the hall, etc.) and their discoveries in many ways come out of that urgency. In these moments it's clear their tone ranges from calming to berating themselves, bitching about others.

The set/design can be as much or as little as is desired, in general there should be a fluidity to the play so it can move from scene to scene.

There are scenes staged outside the office. In The Management's production, the office was kept centralized, it's huge post-it-ed storyboard covered the back wall, but where the carpet ended, on the outskirts, these non-office scenes were staged and popped out further with different lighting.

At times they are watching footage that is projected. Fun with sound is encouraged! The scenes they hear with the Ladies which they describe, can be recreated with audio, and they can listen along, discovering what they can use or gage how what they're presenting is landing.

FOREWORD

When Crystal Skillman first sent me a ten-minute piece she called *Cut*, I was instantly intrigued. The story was about a harrowing day in the life of three reality TV writers. As a more than casual (and often conflicted) viewer of shows featuring tiny pageant contestants and rich-bitch housewives, I loved the idea of exploring the drama—the artistry, even—behind making these types of programs. Beyond the gripping plot, I was drawn to the story's three tightly wound and deeply wounded characters, each on the verge of a decisive moment and each with more to lose than a job. At the core of those few pages were vital themes: regret, forgiveness, love. But what attracted me most as a director to those first ten minutes was the chance to develop this profoundly human and unique play with the brilliant, quirky Crystal. Our theater company, The Management, couldn't wait to get to work on the project, and over the course of eight exhilarating weeks, *Cut* evolved into the dynamic, elegant, and haunting play before you.

We began around the table, each evening reading through the new pages Crystal would send like clockwork each morning. Company members Nicole Beerman and Megan Hill took on the roles of Rene and Collette, respectively (though we had some fun early on experimenting with who should play which character). Joe Varca, long-time friend of The Management, tackled Danno. Through our intense rehearsals and Crystal's keen revisions, the harried writers, charged with the task of re-cutting the season finale of *The Ladies of Malibu* in three hours, became multifaceted individuals. Story-editor Danno longs to successfully re-cut not only the final episode, but he also longs to edit the past, making himself the hero of the story. Rene struggles to control her own fate as masterfully as she plans the storylines of the stars of the reality show. Collette, who logs countless hours of footage ("Vomit and the Coke Party," "Three Way at the Polo Grounds," etc.), tries to prove her worth as both an artist and an adult and fights for a pivotal spot amongst the troubled triumvirate. Each day, the plot grew sharper and the stakes grew higher: Crystal added illuminating flashbacks, slashed entire storylines, and made simple word choices that changed everything. She also created a surprising work of unconventional form and style. The plot skips around in time; at points in the action, all characters are onstage speaking interlocking monologues from different locations; each writer delivers a talking-head type confessional. For me, getting the actors on their feet early and fumbling through dozens of different choices was the most essential step towards figuring out how this world was going to look, sound, and move.

Once we had the rules of *Cut* clearly established, we were ready to get to work on our performance venue at Under St. Mark's—poor in square footage but rich in character. With Crystal, we had transformed the piece. It was now time for our designers to transform the space. The centerpiece of the action is the office itself. Our inspired set designer Kyle Dixon created a room of aggressively bright white pre-fab desks against a backdrop of colored storyboard and cheerful carpet. His design highlighted both the very optimistic and the very temporary nature of their work. Grant Wilcoxen performed miracles with his lighting design, creating discrete and distinct worlds from scene to scene: the lights helped move the story seamlessly from a bustling Barnes and Noble to a trendy L.A. restaurant, from pool-side with Malibu housewife Jessica to a climactic pitch meeting. Sound was also key in establishing the milieu of each scene. Joe Varca and I contextualized the movements with stock muzak transitions (the kind you might hear on any number of reality shows), recorded footage of the haughty and naughty Ladies of Malibu themselves (voiced by not only our cast but the whole production team), and ambient soundscapes (numbing soft rock, passing traffic, ticking clocks). Costumes, designed by Megan Hill, provided insight into the writers—hoody and heels for Collette, jeans and flannel for Danno, dress pants and drape sweaters for Rene—small (and very quick) changes were integral in clarifying past and present moments. Since our beloved theater at Under St. Marks is the size of a postage stamp, we had to push ourselves to be even more economical and inventive with the way space and time worked in this continually shifting story. What we happily discovered is that *Cut*, which feels epic in so many ways, can be performed in just about any type of venue.

Working on *Cut* is like putting together a great puzzle. And Crystal generously gives you few stage directions. My advice is to start experimenting right away with the big staging and design choices and to have fun putting the pieces together. Don't be intimidated when a character begins to narrate the events of the present moment (Collette: "I'm trying to eat my fish tacos from Baja fresh"; Rene: "Running–elevator, shoving other people down, 14th Floor"; Danno: "They want someone to blame. / They want me to choose"). Explore ways to make those scenes active and immediate. Characters take turns soliloquizing next to and even shouting in the faces of others who apparently cannot hear them. Discovering how those moments work alongside the head-on clashes and the more poignant encounters will help you find the sensitive and revealing rhythms of the story. Reality TV is an easy subject to send up. While there's plenty of scandal to go around in this story—and while the writers' own antics rival those of The Ladies themselves—be sure to find the humanity in the characters. Their struggles are at the heart of what makes *Cut* so funny, sad, and true.

In the spirit of adventure and experimentation, The Management endeavored to develop and produce *Cut* with Crystal. I encourage you to go forth in that same spirit as you embark upon telling the story of the damaged and beautiful threesome of Danno, Rene, and Colette. In scene 11—a lighter flashback that comes between an explosive fight and zero hour at the office—Danno opens up to his co-workers (though they are more than co-workers, to call them friends doesn't feel quite right either). He tells them: "working with you is a gift." For me as a director, working on *Cut* was a gift. It was a gift for our company and to our audiences. And it is a gift to any ensemble of intrepid and imaginative artists as well.

– Meg Sturiano
Director, *Cut*
Artistic Director, The Management

To The Management for taking this leap of faith, for Megan, Nicole, Joe, and Meg who lived, breathed, and ate this play, to Fred for being there while I threw all my being into this play day and night, to Kristen Palmer for suggesting me as a match for The Management, for Chris Bannow, Jessica Rothenberg, Natalie Woolams-Torres, Special Sauce Co. and director Heidi Handlesman who hung in there to birth those first ten pages we heard at Jimmy's No. 43, and very special thanks to: Josh Beerman, Jen Schriever, Tara Giordano, Megan McQuillan, Hunter College High School, Kunal Prasad, Jenny Greenfield, Jordana Kritzer, John Wilder, Doric Wilson, and everyone who generously donated to the production. This play is dedicated to all the insane housewives, to all the writers: "real" or not – we share the heartbreak, the love, the late night revelations and may we always...

– Crystal Skillman

1. "SMASH, SMASH"

(Now. Sound of roaring waves in blackout then lights up on:)

DANNO. Blue sky.
Roaring waves.
Sand.
Dolphins.
Motherfucking nature.
Alcoholic drink in a Pineapple.
No one judging you.
Just alone.
No a girl, there's a girl.
In a bikini.
A great girl in a great red bikini.
She looks familiar the way you want her to look.
And she takes you in your hands and just tells you, yeah you, "You'd be so handsome if you'd stop hyperventilating in the bathroom silly."
She says your name as if it matters:
"C'mon *Danno* I forgive you. I love you."
"It's gonna be okay."

It doesn't matter if they are waiting for you to come out of the bathroom.

It doesn't matter when just moments ago your sister who never, ever, never calls is calling but you can't pick up because your super abs big pecks boss is poking through your car window:

"All the other teams working on all the other episodes– they've got them down Danno.
All the other story editors.

DANNO. *(cont.)* In the can.

Done.

And yours.

Unacceptable.

I gave you the finale – I *trusted* you Danno (which is a lie – because *here*, in this place, trust doesn't exist).

We're behind.

You are.

AND YOU NEED TO FIX THIS.

NOW?

DO YOU UNDERSTAND?

DANNO…..?

Roberts shaking his latte-rattle to underscore the urgency and your pocket is on fire and the minute Roberts goes, you check.

No message.

Click.

Just…. *(imitates silence)*

This is so stupid.

Locking myself in here.

This is so menial and small and destructive.

But *I'm* not destructive.

Fuck Rene.

Colette.

They're not your friends.

We work together– that's not even true really.

We work *around* each other.

Hey.

Hey.

Hey.

Remember *The Front Page* with the Masque and Mime players at Drama Camp?

You were so good in that play.

What happened to you?

Your Clark Gable?
Your smile?
Huh, el fucko?
You used to be so good.
You used to care.
Good acting is getting to the truth of the lie.
Get it together.

Reality's written. Reality's planned.
There's no cameras here.
Just you. And you're–.
(He hears a banging on the door.)

I'm not going out there.

*(**COLETTE** rises from her desk, taco in hand.)*

COLETTE. I'm trying to eat my fish tacos from Baja fresh. The ones I couldn't eat at the drive through because Rene has only been back like just a few hours after taking off for two days out of nowhere and I can't believe I even wanted her to be back when she won't even –. She doesn't listen. Care. Just making me so fuckin' nervous I have to take my tacos into the back, hide in the corner of the breakroom, shoving this shit down my throat when it hits me – my dream last night that – one of our housewives this season – the short one with the big face lift eyes and the ratty blonde hair – that lady – Jessica, the one who lives in Malibu with that big mansion, who has that porn tape going around with the 13 year-old, who is always trying to fuck the other ones' husbands, that housewife? She was trying to tell me something in my kitchen over frozen margaritas but she was like sputtering cuz someone had cut her throat, so it was bleeding, it was flapping and she kept trying to keep her head up but it kept slamming back on the table and I look down and I have a knife. The new fucking German pro cutting knife that Bobby, got me at Christmas – I've got in my hands.
I've done it.
This to her.

COLETTE. *(cont.)* Just woke up choking with the words I did hear her politely sputter out:

"*thank you.*"

(**COLETTE** *salsas.*)

I used to salsa dance. Take adult ballet.

Those groups.

They appreciated me.

They loved me.

I used to walk into a room and they'd say, "Look at her! Look at how Colette moves. How she sways. Her eyes. Her ass.

I love her. I love her."

Now it's – "Colette! Rene! Team Meeting!"

(*as* **DANNO**) "They hated the cut. We have to re-cut…a whole new ending…by 6 PM–"

(*as* **RENE**) "TODAY…? That's in three hours!"

(*as* **COLETTE**) "You mean we're not going with the hair pulling and vomiting between the two sisters on the police officers in the parking lot?"

"No. We're not. *Colette.*"

"Then what, *Danno?* What it's it going to be about?"

"I don't know. You're the logger, Colette, find me something."

And if we don't…?

The faces of the crews before us.

The legends of those other loggers and story editors and planners.

(**RENE** *appears, just have banged on the door, pissed at* **DANNO**.)

RENE. I'm right. Totally fucking right you know I am and you can't land this shit on us and then lock yourself in the bathroom Danno! They're going to fire us. Danno? Am I right?

"I don't use that word, Rene."

What word? '*Right*'?

"It's *judgmental*. A *destructive* word."

It's in the fucking dictionary.

"Everything is going to be ok, Rene."

Fuck! Fuck you, Danno!

(RENE lets out a scream of frustration.)

COLETTE. People can be nice.

I've seen it.

Not in my house.

Not here, but I've seen it.

On the street.

Someone, somebody falling and someone stops.

"Are you alright?"

And your boyfriend picks you up, holds you. It's a beautiful thing. It's a beautiful fucking thing.

When I called *my* boyfriend, Bobby, when I told him. He should have jumped in his car, just come the fuck over, instead just:

"It's your choice if you want to have it. I'm not going to stand in the way of anything."

I get so fuckin' mad. I start screaming.

I just throw my cell phone in the street, full on traffic.
Cars just right over.
SMASH.
I'd log that: SMASH!
Squash squash Bobby.

Just like I log all the footage no one else has the time to watch:

"Vomit at the Coke Party"
"Three Way at the Polo Grounds"
"Bitch Slap at the S&M Club"

COLETTE. *(cont.)* Danno's always saying it's like *Our Town* but in the Ladies of Malibu everyone's rich and we narrate their lives.

I don't know what *Our Town* is.

I grew up in a "small town". New York City.
You go back – where I grew up? – and it's like:
"Here's your fucking change."

"Thank you."

"Dog Race & Nude Escort Charity" (Time: 30 minutes 5 seconds)
"Lesbian Tryst on Caribbean Cruise" (Time: 2 hours, 3.5 seconds)

(She makes up their label:)

"Rene Abandons Ship and Comes Back With Her Fancy London Labels on Her Luggage And What Does She Expect?! Welcome Back to the War, The Shitstorm. Population: YOU. Us…."

"Who gets someone a fuckin' knife for Christmas?"

RENE. Sixteen hours ago I was in London. Sixteen hours ago I was walking in Sloane Square. Past people in simple coats and accents and dogs out *running*. People with real jobs, regular smiles, just out in the world.

"One last chance." That's what he said when he called. My husband. So I hopped on a plane, found a sitter. I jumped on that plane.

Like a dog.

"Last chance."

LAX to Heathrow. Heathrow to LAX and I come back to this?

And he's still there.
My husband.
Peter.
On my desk, smiling.

Framed.

Fucking smiling like –.

Colette is dripping fish from her teeth like a seal.

"Did you see the Queen?"

"Everything *is* going to be ok, Rene."

But we both know Danno's lying.

Don't.

Focus.

If they want to blame anyone for this – who's it going to be? Who's going to go?

Cuz if anyone's got to go –

DANNO. If anyone's going to go —

RENE. If it's not going to be me.

COLETTE. Is it going to be you?

RENE. We are missing something.

*(**RENE** goes to the back wall, which is filled with post-its and notes.)*
Story board…my life on fucking pink cue cards….
A perfectly perfect Arc I've written for each lady.
Mandy.
Georgette.
Alexandrea.
Ronny Rose.
Jessica.
Jessica.
JESSICA.

And it's like for the first time in so long Colette and I are both, in a flash:

COLETTE & RENE. "Hand job/Divorce Call in the Jacuzzi!" DANNO!

DANNO. Jacuzzi?

RENE. Jessica!

COLETTE. Jessica!

DANNO. Jessica. Right. Play it! Play!

> *(They look out, up at the screen. Sound: Jessica laughter, the bubbles, the call, the sobbing. They take it all in, watching.* **DANNO** *snaps into action.)*

DANNO. *(cont.)* It can work.
Colette – get me all the footage on Jessica you can, get Jessica's assistant on the phone.
Rene – I need you to do the pick up interview.

> *(They aren't moving)*

C'mon guys. We can do this. *I believe in you.*

RENE. Colette?

COLETTE. Starting now – 2 hours, 45 minutes, 5 seconds.

DANNO. Yes!

COLETTE. If we finish in time –

DANNO. If we cut it right –

RENE. It's about love.

2. "MY ALMOST FUTURE"

*(**DANNO'S** "talking head" confessional.)*

DANNO. I BELIEVE...

What happens in our lives is never chance.
I believe it's because of action.
A year ago, I get on a plane, come out here.
I audition my ass off.
But people look at me and don't see a future.
They see an almost future.
My almost future.

So as much as everyone *hates* reality TV actors – do you know – do you?

That's how that's how you become one.

You come out of an audition where you were so close.
"You remind me of someone –
not *you,* someone else – someone with –
potential talent,
perhaps,
could be,
almost.
No."

So when you come out of that audition you think to yourself: This is it! I've had it and you come out looking like you've had it – desperate. So – BAM!

You get handed a flyer.

(quoting the flyer:) Don't fit in?

Not quite...
Wish you were...
Are you...
Emotional?
Odd looking?
Rambunctious?

DANNO. *(cont.)* High Energy?

Sexy?

And there's an address and you're like why not?
So you go in.

You pretend you're on an island.

You're eating bugs.

You want the gold.

You want the girl.

You backstabber.

You savior.

Bachelor.

And you can't act anything like who you really are, because who the fuck wants to watch that?

You get it.

Make friends with one of the producers – Roberts – insist on watching the rough cut and you can tell it's cut wrong. Because you've worked a million hours at your day job at the Applestore so you can cut it way better, yeah, sorry.

I pissed them off, yeah.

I did, I know this is obsessive but I did, I stayed up and re-cut it, a copy of that shitty footage, came in and showed them the next day.

That show went nowhere, canceled, but six weeks ago Roberts calls me in.

Hands me a card.

Printed with my name.

Danno Collin.

You choose who you are.

3. "FUCK THE KINDLE"

(Then: Six weeks ago. **COLETTE** *is working the booth at Barnes and Noble selling the Nookbook.)*

COLETTE. Motherfucker! Did you hear that old lady? That type there: with those horrible, Sally Jesse glasses –

DANNO. The one in her 40s —

COLETTE. Old, right?! Right before you came up, all snooty pootey pointing her cane, ok, she doesn't have a cane, but all shaking her finger: "It's your fault." "It's because of you the publishing industry is in the toilet. No more books in print!" Like me. Like I am technology. I love being queen of the Nook book booth extolling the virtues of the great Nook book! Look assholes there is no glare! Our picture is bright and clear, fuck the kindle.

DANNO. Look, I just want to upgrade –

COLETTE. Of course, with the upgrade you get a free book so which one do you want...?

DANNO. Oh, god. *Take Back Each Day*, I guess.

COLETTE. The Jessica Rothen *The Ladies of Malibu* tell all book? Get out.

DANNO. Don't judge.

COLETTE. No, I love her. I love how it's such a rip off of the original housewives but even better because it's so much worse. Housewives meets Jersey shore. Disgusting. It's got guts. Honesty. What?

DANNO. Nothing, just seriously?

COLETTE. Like that woman. I want to scream FUCK YOU LADY TO HER FACE – break her Nook book in half, flip everything in this store right at her. But I don't. I shrink. Sweat. Sell. Talk to clueless customers like you when all I want to do is go home, play Wii and drink vodka.

DANNO. Okay well –

COLETTE. And that type? Totally one of those women who hit forty, got a kid from Guatemala, knits in traffic. And that type – totally stuffed his crotch with CDs. From the looks of the hair probably some Best of Poison. You think I don't see? I've got like eyes in the back of my head for this shit. I'm like autistic-ly detail oriented bitch.

DANNO. You really do remind me of someone.

COLETTE. I'm sorry.

(**DANNO** *does a little breathing thing.*)

COLETTE. What the hell is that?

DANNO. Just get nervous sometimes. Started a new job. Keep getting there too early.

COLETTE. You care?

DANNO. Why wouldn't I?

(beat)

COLETTE. Have you been getting your lattes all week here and staring at me because I remind you of some girl?

DANNO. *(The answer is yes but he says:)* No.
You act like my sister.
She's 13, plays violin.

COLETTE. You are weird, dude.

DANNO. Yeah.

(hands her biz card)

COLETTE. Get out you do not work for – the Ladies? With Jessica?

(**DANNO** *nods.*)

What the hell is a Story Editor?

DANNO. You really want to know?

(**COLETTE** *nods.*)

I cut. Cutting is choosing.

(**COLETTE** *stares blankly.*)

Who do you want to be: the hero or the whimp? Hero, right?

(DANNO uses his hands to frame like a camera his "re-cut" shots as he talks.)

Cut to old bitch telling off Colette. Cut to Colette breaking her Nook book. Flipping everything. The crowd. Ohhhhhhh.

COLETTE. And my dialogue we could redo it like:

FUCK YOU LADY!

I am technology!

All of you – go home, play Wii and drink vodka.

I love being Queen of the Nook book!

I'd call that episode: FUCK THE KINDLE BITCH!

DANNO. Yes!

COLETTE. Except that – my boss fired me this morning. "Colette, you have customer relations issues" – I wanted to say "fuck that" as he's letting me go but I take it, come out here and –.

DANNO. What if I wanted to hire you?

COLETTE. I'm pretty sure you'll regret it...Danno.

DANNO. I doubt it. Colette. Can I also get one of those bears with the chocolate?

COLETTE. Ug, why?

DANNO. It's for Rene, the other girl we just hired. To be honest she makes me a little –

COLETTE. Which color?

DANNO. Blue?

4. "MAKE IT PERSONAL"

(**RENE**, *in the hallway.*)

RENE. Running – elevator, shoving other people down, 14th Floor.

And am I crazy or did it look like, or did it really look like out of spite Danno was going to ask Colette to do the interview and what can she do really?

I've caught her – no shit – when she doesn't realize I've come back early from story notes – caught her in the middle of the fucking day in the middle of the room, our office, come back to find her like dancing.

Dancing in the middle of the office, like she doesn't even care.

Well I care.

I fucking care.

(sound: Bing!)

I shove my hand through the door first. At the glass doors of the production office and receptionist, surfing, talking to some security guy who is checking out her ass and she is letting him.

"I need a film crew. Please."

She is not pleased. She is pissed. She grabs a list. A fuckload long list.

"Which day?"

Now.

She laughs. And I see my hand slamming through the glass and ripping off her plastic face until – Ed! ED! Segment producer crew cut classic 50 something Ed, Ipod shuffling, hasn't slept in weeks Ed, I grab him. Too hard, too long. Awkward.

"Pick up interview. Malibu. Jessica Rothen."

"Last chance."

Decide.

Ed.

Please, please, please, please.

Ed silent.

The receptionist: "451 Studios. Born to churn out real entertainment for real people!"

And the clock – *(sound: ticking)*
On the wall.
Each tick that no one can hear but me.
Like a respirator but it's pulling out the air.

Then Ed —he speaks!
"Why not?"

I love Ed. I love Ed more than anything on this earth. Ed is going to get the crew is going to meet me in the parking lot in 15.

Text. My sitter.

"When are you back?"
"I have class."
"You said you'd call after the flight – try to be home after lunch for Celia."

And – I just can't – what would I even say when she asks…?
"When's daddy coming home?"

I'm punching keys, sending, running:
Soon, soon, soon.

2 hours, thirty minutes.

(**RENE** *runs off.* **DANNO** *editing at his desk.*)

DANNO. Rene LEFT me here and she expects what when she comes back – a party?

Just takes the fuck off two days ago– one call from her husband – ex or separated or whatever the hell he is and she just goes?

DANNO. *(cont.)* She listens to *him*.

He needs her, after *he* treated her like...so she just goes...?

I wake up and I'm...I mean who does that...? It's like 2011!!!*

And she did not ask me. She did not ask permission.

Sending a text from the airport ten seconds before you're supposed to take off is not asking permission.

It's post production people! The time that people have to cook, clean, buy spinach, leave their co-workers to go fly off to London –

WE DO NOT HAVE THAT TIME! Sleep here, because this has to air.

This has to live.

(**COLETTE** *on the phone.*)

COLETTE. Almost at 2 hours and twenty minutes, still on hold for Mimi, Jessica's personal assistant. Fucking Danno and Rene – he sends her off to do the interview – I've asked her to bring me like a thousand times –and Mimi – holy shit – picks up.

"Who is this?"

(deepens her voice:) "Colette Ryan. Ladies of Malibu, we need to film a pick up."

Oh my god why am I lowering my voice like that's going to...?

"You're not my contact. Where's Roberts?"

And I don't say Roberts is an asshole and making our lives a living hell and we don't want him to even get wind of what we're doing because if he knew, he'd try to fuck it up. Because even though he wants us to fix it – no one here ever wants anyone to succeed.

Or current year.

"They'll call, they'll confirm but this is important, we need – this afternoon – for the finale."

I'm trying to signal Danno but he's got his Bluetooth in. He wants me to think it's the line producer but I know it's not. Editing at the same time, waving his arms. Lost. I'm alone in this.

Mimi won't let it go:

"Who the fuck are *you?*"

DANNO. I fucking love deleting.

Conducting.

My symphony? Two sisters fighting, vomiting, pulling hair, police officers, pick them up like dolls, fling them into the air – trash – cut and replace with:

Jessica on vacation.
Jessica breakdown at her Botoex Birthday Party.
Jessica with the kid. Correction: Jessica screaming at the nanny about the kid.

Colette took like three seconds to pull up the footage because she knows where they all are by heart which is a little…

The truth is Colette sneaks out footage. She emails shit home so she can watch it, burns CDs. They know she does it – starting searching bags in the office.

She would have been let go then if Rene hadn't –.

Don't even think about Rene. Don't even think she came back for you.

COLETTE. "Hellooooo… "Who the fuck are you? Who the fuck is Colette?"

(**RENE** *at the elevator.*)

RENE. Elevator opens.
Production crews. Christ we must have the only fat people in LA.

RENE. *(cont.)* And – its Roberts, fuck! – latte guzzling Roberts in his EP casual "we're all friends here until we're not" sweatsuit power trip and flip flops.

Right there.

Looking at me.
Like he knows.
Like Danno told him.
They're old friends right?

Coming back from Baja Fresh — Colette going on something about "sometimes you have to make big choices" but she won't even listen to anything you try to tell her – and there you see Roberts with Danno in the parking lot.

And in your head you can hear – and you can't tell if it's paranoid or real but you can hear what he's saying to Danno.

Elevator doors closing – I can't.

Head for the stairs. Roberts stays on, probably didn't even see me, but in my head follows me down the hall.

"Yeah, Danno told me everything about you. How you like it. Did you like it *honey*...?"

(**RENE** *exits.*)

COLETTE. "Who the fuck is Colette?"

You want to see who I am?

I take the phone and smash it into my screen right into my laptop.

Everything everyone has googled from the past three weeks.

British Airways, Flights to the UK, a.k.a Rene

"Light a Stress Candle/Learn to Breath" Hippie Bull-shit, a.k.a. Danno

Abortion Pill Online brought to you now live!

(**COLETTE** *reenacts what she learned about ordering*

the pill online. For some reason this voice she might use seems kinda ghetto/rapper-y...?)

Yo my main bitch Colette! If you fucked up pregnant less than 63 days
1 Pack of 3 abortion pills can be fedexed your way!
We accept Credit Cards and Online Checks, bitch, so don't hold out on da monies.

That's right honey, I know you got Bobby's credit card number that you wrote down when you got the movie tickets, and uh-huh Black Swan what the fuck was that all about right? Some hot ass masturbation stabbing lesbian dancing motherfucking awesome shit!

You got wings?

You ready to spin and thrust and launch into your motherfucking future of non-pregnant perfection???

Flip that mastercard, put down that bastard bobby's stolen security code – press send and FLY MOTHER FUCKER!

But LISTEN bitch! Orders received before 4 P.M Eastern Time (U.S.) are processed and shipped that day. Orders received after 4 P.M are processed and shipped the next morning so if you ordered yesterday that is today!

(She drops voice, becomes herself again, as:)

You see yourself?
Opening the bottle?
Taking out a big pill.
Blue.
Down your throat and imagine!
Follow it down.
It will make you the way you were before.
Empty.

Which is funny if you think about it and what's even funnier is when you faint and Danno makes you leave to go to the doctor and the doc is so handsome, it's

COLETTE. *(cont.)* disturbing, like he's on one of those hospital soap shows and he's rubbing your back like you're a tiny hamster and then he's like, "When was your period?" and I'm like seriously you think I have time to figure that out and he's like pee in a cup just in case and he's like it's really good you did that.

Because you are.

I am.

DANNO. An argument about who's going to pay the check can be cut the same as an argument about an affair.
About hate can be love.
Joy.
That's the point. Do what you have to. To get what you want.

Cut Colette from the scene.

(COLETTE exits.)

Bring Rene in.

(RENE runs in.)

What I say to her when she walks in this morning:
(to RENE) You can't just run off whenever you want to without – fuck!

But instead of:

RENE. Fuck you Danno!

DANNO. Replace!

RENE. You're right. Thank you.

DANNO. Cut Colette back in.

(COLETTE comes back in.)

COLETTE. You're the best Danno!

DANNO. And it's great – we finish, we give them the cut and THEY LOVE IT! ME!

COLETTE. Genius!

RENE. Inspired!

COLETTE. You've won!

DANNO. Yes!

(They clap, then turn, snapping back to reality: **COLETTE** *returns to her desk, on the phone.* **RENE** *exits.* **DANNO** *"turns" on himself, snapping back to editing:)*

Get it together, Danno.

COLETTE. Two hours left!

DANNO. My sister she hasn't…I can't reach her.
Been trying on the headset but I can't keep –
(**RENE** *in the stairwell.*)

RENE. Push the door open into the stairwell.

COLETTE. Answer Mimi.

"Who is Colette?" She's the loser Rene walks in on puking her guts out in the bathroom after lunch.
And she knows.
She just knows.
I am.
And she just…going on about herself and then:

"You shouldn't do that here. Everyone can tell."

Walks out.

And when that package gets here, my pill, when I….
I'll be picturing her face when I swallow you bet. Fly motherfucker!

DANNO. Why can't it be simple?
Like Jessica being picked up by her plastic surgeon husband at Hooters.
Rene she's got photos of her from when Jessica was just…a kid.
Midwest.
And her – no shit – braces, prom, pregnant…. Wedding.

Rene…

There is joy in her.
I've seen it.
Only once.

RENE. Peter – when he took me to Heathrow, just:
"Go ahead. Blame me for what I've done. But you need to forgive.
If you love me.
I need an answer, Rene.
Can you change?
Can you be the woman I need you to be?"

And who the hell would that be?

COLETTE. I am not losing this call.

RENE. I text Colette I'm coming up – the crew is waiting in the parking lot.

COLETTE. Now she needs me after she treated me? I'd log that: BAD FUCKING TIMING RENE!

RENE. Colette isn't answering.

COLETTE. You think I'm going to help you now? I am getting this interview. I am going to win!

RENE. At the door. Emergency Exit to our floor. Locked. Shit. Shit. Ed is waiting. Roberts. COLETTE! COLETTE! Open the door!

COLETTE. Because I've got guts and I'll show you – all that matters is what Mimi wants, I cut in my head what I need to do.

Danno taught me – make it personal.

Mimi. "Helloooo…is anyone still there?"

(*DANNO turns, listening in.*)

"Mimi…
We hate to call.
Go into overtime
But we feel
So strongly
About ending with a clear perspective of Jessica's side
What Jessica thinks
Feels

We want what's best for her

Because we know she hasn't been featured as much as she should be

Not like those *other* ladies

Her book sales may have gone down

But

If we do this, *now*, she will be

Better than those other ladies

It will be *her* story."

RENE. COLETTE!

DANNO. – Do you have it? What is she saying? Less than 2 hours.

RENE. Let me in!

COLETTE. *(as Mimi)* "Jessica'll be by the pool. You have thirty five minutes."

RENE. Now!

DANNO. Colette – do you have it?

COLETTE. "Helloooo....?"

DANNO. Colette!

RENE. Open the door!

COLETTE. *(to Mimi)* "We're – NO.

I'm on my way."

5. "THE SECRET"

*(**RENE'S** "talking head" confessional.)*

RENE. I BELIEVE...

The first time someone besides my husband found out what I do *now*, that I got hired for *this* – was my parents. A few weeks ago. At their new house with the new dogs. Connecticut. Easter.

My husband just outs me. He, for whatever reason just:

"Rene's new job it's for reality TV. That housewives show."

It's a like bomb landed on the table.
It's like roaches exploded out of the roasted lamb and stuffing and crawled up the table and ate my face.
Their *look*.

"Why would they need writers."
Those women are really stupid. You watch them?"

(She imitates her parents:)

Mom – Sauvignon.
Dad – chin.

"What happened to the screenplay? The novel?"

And these are *not* the words your parents say to you but these *are* the words they mean:
You are the New Yorker.

You are steaks on Sunday.
You are nice to the neighbors who laugh when you say you are an artist.
You are the trust fund until it's decided you're no longer worth it.
You are Yale grad.
You are clothes napkins.
You are china plates.
Silver.

You are *us*.

You were supposed to be.

But you sit here and you are changing and we don't know what trash you'll be.

And your own daughter.

Your Celia?

Aren't you afraid what she'll grow up to be?

Because if this is where you're going,

God forbid…

God.

And it strikes, the part of me I've protected so long.

I'm just…I'm open, my arms are open and God forbid you say the words I've been waiting for you to say my whole life:

I BELIEVE. I REALLY BELIEVE. IN YOU.

Plate. Knife. Cut.

"It's just a job."

While inside me my heartbeat:

FUCK YOU.

FUCK YOU.

FUCK YOU.

Because I hold my daughter and I am afraid.

She'll be like me.

6. "YOU KNOW JAWS?"

(Three weeks ago. **COLETTE** *and* **RENE** *cramped against a wall in the bar of a fancy restaurant.)*

COLETTE. Are you okay? You don't look ok. I'm sorry it's taking so long. Fuck! Right, fuck! Bobby he'll get us a table – I'm just glad you came.

RENE. You have three seconds.

*(***RENE*** looks at her iPhone, timing her.)*

COLETTE. Okay. Shit. Shit I mean –

RENE. Done.

*(***RENE*** starts to go.)*

COLETTE. I'm sorry. I never meant to get you in trouble– thank you. My mom thinks that means: dinner, fancy restaurant. Of course for her that means Pina Coladas at BBQ's –

*(***RENE*** tries to go again.)*

Please. Please. Please. Please. Please. Don't –

RENE. Why do you take that Jessica shit home with you?

COLETTE. I don't. I don't know. I didn't know they would search our bags. I can't believe you said it was yours. I can't believe they believed you.

RENE. Why?

COLETTE. We all know you never make a mistake.

You're so good at this reality shit.

When I came out here to open a dance studio. OH MY GOD THAT SOUNDS LIKE THE DUMBEST THING EVER.

But you – you have something you can do, I don't even know how you –

RENE. Oh give me a break.

COLETTE. You think I'm stupid, I get it.

RENE. You know Jaws.

COLETTE. Some shark eats naked ladies. What does that have to do with…?

RENE. Storyplanning? It's Jaws. Perfect beginning, middle and end.

COLETTE. I don't…

RENE. Pick anybody.

COLETTE. Ohhhh…Danno.

RENE. Good one. Small Town is like 451 Studios. One guy Danno. Biggest fear: not being accepted, like being scared of the water. Shark is in the water.

COLETTE. This time it's personal.

RENE. Right. So he has to face his fear – go in the water. But scene by scene we discover what he wants.

COLETTE. To blow the fucking shark up!

RENE. To blow the fucking shark up.

COLETTE. Oh but like what's the shark for Danno?

RENE. See? Now that's. That's philosophy.

COLETTE. It's family.

RENE. What do you mean?

COLETTE. He's always googling flights home but never goes out. His sister, plays her tracks from her orchestra – no shit – that he put into his iTunes but he never calls her.

RENE. So – pick scenes to show that conflict.

COLETTE. Like trying to do yoga on his lunch break in his office while burning incense, but coming out more stressed than ever.

RENE. "I believe!' I believe! I believe!"
That's good, that's –

*(**COLETTE**, continuing the "Jaws" storyboarding game:)*

COLETTE. Oh and for you it's your kid right? That's what you care about. And your husband – I see him all the time in that Mercedes commercial.

RENE. He wants to do more than that. Just went to London. Acting fellowship, he'll be back soon.

COLETTE. You must miss him.

RENE. I really do have to go okay? Tell Bobby thanks for –

COLETTE. Why did you do it? Stick up for me?

RENE. We've got three more weeks together. I don't want to start over with someone new.

COLETTE. Noooo. You like me.

RENE. Just –

COLETTE. What?

RENE. Just stop taking that shit home to watch and you'll be fine, ok?

COLETTE. Rene?

If it ever does really go bad, and they're gonna…you'll let me know right.

I don't want to be one of those people taken down the hall, into a room. Get your coat. Get an email kind of thing.

I want to go in my own way. Like…have respect you know. Does that make sense?

(beat)

RENE. How about, I'll wave.

COLETTE. So it's like I'm going on a trip! Something nice.

RENE. Yeah. Like that.

COLETTE. Danno – I know this is weird. Something about the way he says your name.

RENE. You are…

I do.

COLETTE. What?

RENE. Like you. Colette.

COLETTE. Oh shit! Look Bobby got us a table!! Yay!

7. "THE PUSH"

(Now, picking up from Scene 4.)

DANNO. You got the interview?

COLETTE. Jessica's waiting for us by the pool.

DANNO. The crew.

COLETTE. Downstairs. Rene texted.

DANNO. Where is she…?

COLETTE. You could send me.

(RENE walks in.)

I'd do a great job.

DANNO. Rene –

RENE. Yeah, *Colette*, you'd be great. You just don't know how to open doors huh?

COLETTE. I –

RENE. You do not speak. You are lucky a janitor let me in. A very *kind* person.

DANNO. I don't know what you're –

RENE. Forget it. I'm ready to go just –

COLETTE. I've got everything I pulled for Jessica here.

DANNO. Great – Rene – use it to edit on the way if you don't get what you need. Are you –

RENE. I'm fine.

DANNO. Colette give Rene the disc, you can help me with –

COLETTE. No. I should go on the interview.

DANNO. Rene always does pick ups you know that.

COLETTE. Why?

DANNO. Look, I get it Colette- we'll get you out there, put you on other interviews next time but this – getting Jessica to spill her guts in her own words over what happened – this will put the whole re-cut into context. Without this, we're –. But we will – Rene will get this and everything will be —

COLETTE. But I know Jessica better than anybody.

RENE. It's a fantasy. You watch her and imagine you know her. There's a difference.

COLETTE. How would you know? You treat us like shit.

RENE. You have no idea what you're talking about so shut it – I'm not kidding you, Colette.

COLETTE. You can't tell me what to do and if you'd just –

RENE. What?

COLETTE. Sometimes you just fucking need someone, Rene. It wouldn't hurt you to admit that.

RENE. And how would you know? You won't listen to anyone unless they act like you! Like your insecure wack-a-doo self – like: are you mad at me? Do you like me? Are we friends. I *need* to talk to someone. I *need* a friend.

COLETTE. You can't admit I do anything right. That I can be better than you!

DANNO. Leave her alone.

COLETTE. Why? Because you're fucking her? You give her the most important jobs to do because Rene is always sooo important –

RENE. Oh my…

DANNO. Watch it, Colette.

COLETTE. It's true – isn't it?

RENE. You have no idea what's going on with me. No idea what I'm going through.

DANNO. And what is going on with you? We'd all really like to know.

RENE. In thirty minutes I'm supposed to be there! Danno. We do not have time for this.

DANNO. No, we don't.
Give her the disc, Colette.

COLETTE. I'm not giving her shit. Either of you.

RENE. Do you want us all to be let go? Stop being a fucking child.

COLETTE. I'm the child? You're the bully! Both of you. All you do is push me around. You'd push me down to the ground if you could.

DANNO. Listen to me –

COLETTE. No. You – don't have time to take your sister's phone calls and then try desperately to get her back on the line. You can't treat me like you treat her and your sister, like me, can take care of herself I'm sure.

RENE. Don't talk about things you don't understand, Colette. And you can't just —

COLETTE. Yes I can! Because nothing is private with any of us. All I do is listen to the shit you tell me– like I'm a kid. I'm not. Not here. Not in this place and you have no right to be angry with me.

DANNO. Enough! Rene go – Colette just – be quiet and –

COLETTE. No! I won't until you both treat me like –. I deserve. Don't I deserve – respect?

(The word "respect" lands like a bomb in the room.)

*(**RENE** crosses to her.)*

RENE. *Respect?* Colette, honey. We've been together for six weeks trying to make sense of other women snatching little doggies in Gucci bags away, falling down drunk at grand balls, ripping off each other's bras and hair in parking lots. Over failed marriages, that were probably real once, even for all the fake money shit, there was probably something before our cameras got there. The time we've spent together we've spent together to create some kind of story about the last good moment in peoples sad, sad lives and I'm sorry you got yourself pregnant but I don't know you, Colette, so I can't answer that question.

*(**COLETTE** throws the footage at **RENE**.)*

COLETTE. Here's your fucking footage.

"Jessica Smoking Pot at the Battered Women Benefit."

"Jessica Crying After Losing her Dog in her Backyard for a Half Hour!"

It's yours.

DANNO. You're pregnant?

COLETTE. I fainted in front of you. What did you think Danno? Are you that lost that you can't see anything that's really – fuck.

DANNO. Colette!

(**COLETTE** *waves* **DANNO** *off, goes to the fire escape or downstairs, out in the hall.*)

RENE. I didn't mean to – to act like –

DANNO. But you did.

RENE. No – that's not who I –.

DANNO. Yes it is! Just admit that it is! For Christ's sake, stop running off – stay for one fucking moment and –

RENE. "Just be myself?"

Like one of your speeches.

What you tell all the ladies before we film them.

"Be *real*. Because where else in the world could you be where people care what you think, what you say, what you do, what you feel? Where else will you be *loved* like that?"

You want me to confess to you Danno?

No. Not today. Not when I back come to –.

DANNO. And why did you? Because the last time we talked, /really talked was –

RENE. /If we're going to make it, I have to –

DANNO. Right. Go.

RENE. When I get back we will, we'll…we will –.

(**RENE** *goes.*)

DANNO. Fuck!

(*Pop music blares. The three of them all start to dance in a very fucked up way which segues into…*)

8. "GIFT"

(Then. A few days ago. The song continues to play. **DANNO** *passes drinks around the office . They are drunk and excited.)*

DANNO. Yeah! We are not working overtime!

COLETTE. Yeah!!

RENE. But – we're missing something. Something was really brewing with Jessica.

DANNO. Something is always brewing. You think *they* aren't tired?

COLETTE. Right. Throwing furniture and pulling out hair is tiring.

DANNO. And we need this. I need this.

RENE. Well – nice, but I've got to go, the –

DANNO & COLETTE. Sitter.

RENE. Nice. But seriously –

DANNO. Sure well. Uh, we need to…

COLETTE. Oh! Right!

*(***COLETTE*** turns out the lights. They bring her a treat, sans candle but in the spirit of having one.)*

RENE. Oh you've got to be…

*(***DANNO & COLETTE*** sing Happy Birthday.)*

DANNO. Make a wish.

RENE. This is insane.

COLETTE. C'mon.

RENE. A Yodel?

DANNO. Yodels in LA! I can't believe I found them!

RENE. Thanks Minnesota boy.

DANNO. I'm sure you have delicious snacks in your hometown of…

RENE. New York.

Chicago.

Connecticut.

My parents like new houses.

COLETTE. What the hell do they do?

RENE. Art Dealers.

(**COLETTE** *laughs.*)

They are. What?

COLETTE. Nothing.

DANNO. Guys, guys I just have to – you have worked your ass off. I swear to god Rene you're why they gave us the finale. They loved what you pulled out of Episode two and Colette — you finding that bit about that red head telling her psychic of that dream that clearly is the whole reason she hates her sister. Genius. Seriously. You've both been...great. And so, a moment.

(*He holds up his beer toasting as does* **COLETTE**.)

COLETTE. A moment.

RENE. Yes.

(**RENE** *only raises up her iPhone to "toast" not looking up from texting. Beat.*)

DANNO. I never said anything but you know why...when you answered the ad – why I said yes?

RENE. Uhhhh...

DANNO. "The Last Goodbye."

COLETTE. What the hell is that.

RENE. Get out. You read that.

DANNO. Read it? Used it to audition all the time. Seriously. Love that play.

RENE. I'm flattered.

DANNO. Seriously – she won awards and stuff for it. I didn't want to play favorites, you know embarrass you.

RENE. Embarrass me.

DANNO. I just like it so much, I didn't want to you know, geek out on you.

COLETTE. No shit, why didn't you say anything.

RENE. I was like nineteen. It was like a teen contest thing.

COLETTE. I never won anything.

DANNO. Maybe we'll win an Emmy.

COLETTE. Don't even joke.

RENE. We don't exist.
Unscripted programming remember?
When the credits come up our names will be there at the end in a lump.

DANNO. First time I saw it come up like that – *(unsaid: my name)* – and oh this is so stupid, I felt sick. I knew that was always the deal right, stupid just I always thought back when I was…
Like…
I'd get this role.
Small, seriously not like…
But when it scrolled down.
I'd have a name.
I'd be like that was me.
I did that.

RENE. It isn't stupid.

DANNO. Now you-tube me and you know what comes up? That audition for Survivor. They posted it. So.

(It's a little sad. **COLETTE** *and* **RENE** *jump in.)*

COLETTE. Yes, and…there's been such a fever for it.

RENE. Danno your pretending to eat bugs while stuck in a pit was so genius.

COLETTE. Genius!

RENE. Inspired!

COLETTE. We have nominate you…

RENE. And it's an honor just to be nominated…

COLETTE. And you've won!

*(**RENE** grabs the blue bear in the office, presents it to him.)*

RENE. The International Globe of Supreme Best Actor!

COLETTE. Supreme! You're the best Danno!

DANNO. Thank you, thank you, ladies.
To be here with you.
Celebrating this.
It's a gift.
Working with you is a gift.

RENE. You're right. Thank you.

DANNO. You should stay. You can stay.

*(**COLETTE** pumps up the music – something like Lady Gaga. They all laugh, make fun of song, sing, dance.)*

9. "SWALLOW"

(Now. **RENE** *at Jessica's house.)*

RENE. Respect? I'll show you respect.
With Ed, the crew, up the long driveway,
Jessica's mansion is gleaming.
Jessica's standing right there when we pull up.
Waiting for me.

*(***COLETTE*** in the parking lot.)*

COLETTE. It hits me the minute I get away from them
Fresh air.
The trees lining the parking lot.
What separates our Studio from the world.
An hour used to be a lot of time.
Now it's a countdown.
Coming towards me.
Getting faster as it goes.
Kicking up dust even though it's pavement.
Like a horror movie.
Turning
Fedex truck.
It stops.
Man getting out.
And I'm –.
I can barely walk.
But I do – up to him.

Do you have anything for a Colette?
Colette. Colette Ryan.

He holds up – a package.

*(***DANNO*** struggling to finish the last stages of editing. His Bluetooth is in.)*

DANNO. My sister still not picking up.

I call home.

"Hello?"

My dad's voice, raspy

But sober.

Dad – I don't have time to talk about the weather, repairs on the house – where's Sarah?

"Sarah? She goes off sometimes. She comes back. She always does."

But I can tell – he's worried.

RENE. Housewife Jessica is shielding her eyes and there's some kind of male guard friend – the one she gave the hand job to looking smug.

The film crew's all set up.

We're in the chairs by the figure eight pool the size of ten SUVs.

And she's smiling.

DANNO. "Sarah was taking her meds right?"

"Danno. You know she never did, not really."

And I'm like did you even call the police.

RENE. I'm like ok: we're going to cut to this interview right after you get the divorce call from your husband, so you shouldn't be smiling ok? And I swear to god. That grin, it doesn't come off and she's like what? And I'm like: THIS IS LIKE EMOTIONAL SHIT OK. It's time to let it hang out. And she's like:

"I'm getting a lot of money. The settlement."

For a second I see my daughter: I see her bank account.

Zero.

Maybe Jessica you can talk more?

DANNO. Dad – Did you call the police?

"Yeah."

COLETTE. I walk into the lobby.

Package in my hands.

Cold.

Holding it, I'm someone else.

RENE. Maybe – Maybe you can share what it's like when the man you love tells you are nothing like who he fell in love with? How all the affairs were your fault because you're hard and uncaring, even though you paid his fucking air fare to London with your shit job. About how in the middle of the night you cross the earth and right here – last chance – but all the time you feel Danno…holding you.

Jessica she just:

"You have to be your best self, pick yourself up, be nice to yourself in times of tragedy."

There are no tears, no…

And I hate myself – I hate myself when my first thought is we'll have to cut in Colette's earlier footage of Jessica crying after losing her dog in her backyard for a half hour.

Because the audience will need that.

They want that.

(breaking:)

I respect myself for knowing I can do that.

I so fucking respect myself it's –.

*(***RENE*** looses it, exits completely.)*

DANNO. "Dad. Sarah didn't say…she didn't tell you where she was going?"

"Just what she always says…

"What? What does she…?"

"To find you."

"I hope you… that you make it. Out there. Take care son."

Click.

*(***COLETTE*** is now in the elevator like ***RENE*** once was.)*

COLETTE. Elevator.

I'm pressing up.

Doors closing.

A hand! Ed – pushing open the door.

He rushes in, the crew.

They have it – the interview.

I grab it.

Where's Rene?

They don't know.

She didn't come up with them.

There's no time to go back down.

Roberts secretary is texting me.

The presentation – they're starting.

Danno!

(COLETTE races off.)

(DANNO. is almost finished, trying to lose himself in the work.)

DANNO. Connecting – the last of it –

Shadows of the trees on the beach, the beautiful houses, people until we get to Jessica.

The what's going to happen next.

(imitates:) "Dum. Da. Dum."

Music falls into place, turns into the orchestra in my mind.

Chellos

Violin –

I hear…

One held out note – Symphony No. 3…Beethoven – was it Beethoven – the last time I heard her –.

(He forces himself to go back to the footage, trying to "orchestrate.")

Jessica takes off her bikini top.

She gets in.

She…

*(**DANNO** stops working. **DANNO** looses control. **DANNO** does serious damage to anything around him, throws, kicks, screams, hits the wall. **COLETTE** comes in.)*

Rene.

COLETTE. She didn't come up but if you want to make the meeting it's started…you have to –

*(**COLETTE** holds out the footage. Survival clicks in. **DANNO** grabs the cut. Lights blast onto **DANNO** as he runs out –)*

10. "CLOSING"

DANNO. Down the hall.

> Melting between bodies.
> Clutching what we're to present, Rene's cut of the interview, past:
> Sets.
> Cameramen.
> Crews.
> EPs.
> Showrunners.
> Assistants.
> Delivery men.
> Receptionist by the plant.

> She holds me there.
> The doors are closed.
> The doors are shut.
> They open.
> A crack.
> I slide in like a thief.

> Roberts now out of flip flops and no more latte, is sitting and the other showrunners.
> Everyone in charge of each team, the whole goddamn force behind *The Ladies of Malibu*.
> All men.
> All suits.

> No one is happy.

> They keep the door open as if it's a pit, as if the others can watch and see what the lions do to someone who doesn't belong in their world.

> For the first time I understand why my father drinks.

> They make sure I understand the notes, where "they're coming from."
> That I understand I have failed.

So they ask: What have I done to correct it?

What do I have to show them?

It starts with the pitch, it always does and I do.
My body is moving.
There is an orchestra, and my arms, it's like nothing I've done before, the way my body is, I'm fully here and grand and simple and grounded and real.
Giving them the Jacuzzi divorce call.
Because I care.
Because it's personal.
Because this is my *life*.

And they're not…I can't tell.
But they're listening.

They are.

I show them the recut ending.

(*As* **DANNO** *shows the executives the cleaned-up footage they discovered at the start, we hear the drama that's unfolding for Jessica in the jacuzzi:*)

The music.
Dum. Da. Dum.
The bubbles.
The handjob.
The call.
The crying.

They are still watching, they're still…

It cuts out…
They look to me.
It's scary but at the same time they look like children.
I have to show them,
I have to lead them.

"But all of that will end with one final interview.
Jessica by the pool.
It's rough."

DANNO. *(cont.)* I press play.

(We hear Jessica crying. A dog whimpering in the background. Jessica may call out for her "sweetie".)

And what was almost.

What was almost is becoming real.

It's good.

Holy shit.

Jessica – the way she's crying.

Her hair falling.

It's really, really fucking good.

And of course I know, I know it's cut from some other scene, she did such a close up, we can't even see the clothes are different, but what Rene has done is brilliant.

Brilliant!

Because it doesn't matter she has them.

I HAVE THEM.

Jessica – after all that sobbing, heaving:

(Sound – we hear Jessica: "You have to be your best self, pick yourself up, be nice to yourself in times of tragedy.")

"It's good."

BUT –

(He is caught.)

"This can never happen again."

"The time."

"The money."

They want someone to blame.

They want me to choose.

Who.

I hear my words.

About Rene's brilliance, about Colette's eyes in the back of her head.

DANNO. *(cont.)* About their sensitivity and love and honesty even when they're angry with me just – all the ways they put themselves in what they do and how they make me who I am on my lowest of days and *why* –

Why couldn't she stay?

Words in my head but the only word that escapes from my mouth:

Rene.

They say they understand.
After what happened with her mistakes which was Colette's and before I can say anything –

Their arms are around me
They always knew I had…I was something.
And in me, the doors are closing.
Something is closing.

So I can pretend.
That I don't feel my phone….
And know it's her.
My sister.
Calling and I just…

I just let myself feel their arms around me and…
It's almost like…almost.

11. "LET ME"

(Then, picking up from the birthday party.)

DANNO. Rene. You want a ride. You gotta go home?

RENE. Right, right. Where's Colette?

DANNO. She left like ten minutes ago. Oh, you are wasted.

RENE. I am…wasted.

(They laugh.)

DANNO. You are.

RENE. And I am *old*.

DANNO. Oh, c'mon.

RENE. You didn't really use my play for auditions did you?

DANNO. Yeah.

RENE. Oh god, and what – was I graduating college??

DANNO. I'm just a few years younger.

RENE. And those few make all the difference.

DANNO. I kept using it – it got me into grad.

RENE. You went to grad.

(He unbuttons his shirt which reads: N.Y.U.)

N.Y.U. Must have been a good audition.

Do it.

(He prepares to audition. Looks up – starts, tries – then breaks laughing, she does too.)

DANNO. Don't even, c'mon.

RENE. Seriously.

DANNO. You don't ask a chef to just – cook on demand.

RENE. You do on Top Chef.

DANNO. And as you throw back in my face so often "there are no cameras here so just calm down, Danno."

RENE. I say that?

DANNO. All the time. And I mean I don't ask you to just whip off a new play or film –

RENE. I was a kid –

*(Makes fun of it – her own writing while it's clear **DANNO** knows it well.)*

"Hey, hey, hey.

I know you're…

That this is…

And every time we wake up we think it's the last goodbye but it's just begun.

If you just let me.

Let me love you.

And I will, I'll – "

To write about love like I knew –

DANNO. I believe it.

It feels…

It's honest.

Love. It's weird.

My parents – they never even got married.

They just fucked on top of some mountain in Arizona.

Had me and later my sister and their lives had meaning.

They named her Willow.

I'm pretty sure they were drunk when they came up with that.

The minute she could – she switched to her middle name:

Sarah. Left her there with them. Could tell things were bad.

But…

I came here.

RENE. Love. It gets complicated and then there's kids.

DANNO. Celia, right?

I heard you when we had to stay late and we ordered out from Chin Chin. Singing into the phone.

(Gently, sincerely imitates her singing to her child:)

"Goodnight my baby, goodnight my honey..."
Something, something.
Celia.

*(***RENE** *smiles.)*

I really. I'd like to be. A dad. Maybe. Someday.

RENE. We should go.

DANNO. Rene?

RENE. Yeah?

DANNO. Why did you stick up for Colette?

RENE. The way they were yelling. I saw her face. Something in me knew – I had to.

DANNO. That's a good thing to have.

RENE. Is it?

DANNO. It is. A beautiful thing.

You want to go.

We have to get the lights and do the lock and I am drunk and I have to – pee. Too many Stellas. Be right back. Ok?

RENE. Ok.

DANNO. Ok.

*(***DANNO** *leaves,* **RENE** *takes out her phone, dials.)*

RENE. C'mon.
C'mon.

(Her husband doesn't pick up. She hangs up. Her phone rings.)

Peter. Peter. I've been trying to call you back, I've been trying to. This is what you say to me? This is how you tell me it's over? "Last chance?" Leave me messages about…I hear her laughing in the…Who's this one? What's her name? Who the fuck is she Peter? I don't give a shit. You tell me. No, I didn't mean. Oh god, oh god, I can't…FUCK!

(She hangs up. **DANNO** *has come in, seen this.* **RENE** *realizes.)*

RENE. I don't want to hear what you have to say right now, ok?

(A beat, a split second. **DANNO** *"prepares" again – starts to perform Rene's monologue from the play she wrote years ago but it's natural, real. It hurts* **RENE** *to hear, but also brings her joy, unfolds her in a way we've never seen before. It's like the greatest gift anyone could give her.)*

DANNO. Hey.

Hey.

Hey.

I know you're…

That this is…

But whatever this is…

It is…

And I might be everything you hate, everything that makes you angry and cry.

But I'll be everything that makes you hold me.

That makes you run to me.

And maybe it's because we break up every week.

Every day.

Every hour.

And every time we wake up we think it's the last good-bye but it's just begun.

If you just let me.

Let me love you.

And I will, I'll…

(They are very close now. **RENE** *kisses him aggressively, intensely. He does too. There is nothing gentle about it.)*

12. "WAVE"

(**COLETTE'S** *"talking head" confessional.*)

COLETTE. I BELIEVE God is a shitty producer.
He doesn't know how to cut anything right. He just lets the drama hang out, no context.
We make the context.
We imagine what people see themselves as, want to see themselves as.
People want authenticity.
They ask: Who are you when moments of crisis-tragedy-pain-suffering-loss-joy hits!
Who are you, what comes out, what do you do, say where do you go?

I take the footage home because I make that happen for them.
Their big houses, their cars.
I make who they are possible.
How they breath, how they look naked.
I *know* them.
I made them.
My family.

Cutting is choosing.

Jessica, what I'd imagine she would say: "I'm happy you're pregnant. Colette."
She'd make me a margarita.

(*The lights shift.* **COLETTE** *stands or moves, present, in the office:*)

I rip open the package.
Take out the bottle.
Take out a pill.
Go to the bathroom.
Then…and it's not a choice, it's *instinct* – it's me! Just… like a fucking avalanche.
All the pills.

The toilet water sprays when I throw them in and I don't even care.

Danno's text.
Meeting's over.
You're Safe.
I write back.
"Rene?"

"Go home Colette."

And I don't know why.
I just –
I go out on the fire escape.

*(**RENE** is seen in the parking lot. She takes out her phone, texts to her husband: "NO." **COLETTE** sees her:)*

Rene's she's – in the parking lot.
At the lobby door as if she wants to…but can't.
She sees me and I want to –.
But all I can is –

*(**COLETTE** waves. **RENE** sees. She waves back. **COLETTE** goes into the now empty office, starts shutting down. **RENE** waits.)*

13. "THE LAST GOODBYE"

(Now. **DANNO** *comes into the parking lot to go to his car, maybe even still looking at his phone. Looks up –* **DANNO** *is stunned –* **RENE** *is there waiting.)*

RENE. Hey.

DANNO. Hey.

RENE. Before you say anything I know I'm…

DANNO. I'm sorry. But there's nothing I can –

RENE. I know.

DANNO. You didn't come back up.

RENE. Peter.
 I texted him while I was out here.
 Told him it was over.

DANNO. Why?

RENE. I had to.
 It's better for Celia.
 That's what I keep telling myself but –

DANNO. It is.
 I'm sorry.
 So.
 You're alright?

*(***RENE** *might nod.* **COLETTE** *leaving work, enters, sees them. A beat.)*

RENE. Colette – I know earlier you tried to – but I think you should –

*(***COLETTE** *hugs* **RENE**. **RENE** *lets her.* **DANNO** *grows angry, guilty, pissed.)*

DANNO. Wow this is –. This is –.

RENE. What?

DANNO. Forget it.

(turns to go)

COLETTE. Where are you going? You can't just –

DANNO. WHY? What do I owe you? Either of you? This is. Today. What happened. It is what it is. And I'm sorry it didn't work out with your husband, I'm sorry you're pregnant, I'm sorry my sister –.

She won't leave a message.
She needs me.
I don't know where she is.

(beat)

I wanted to save us.
I wanted you to stay.
Cutting is choosing.
But the reality is I can't –
I can't –

*(**RENE** goes to him, touches him. Her words, a gift.)*

RENE. But you can choose.

*(**RENE** looks at him, making sure he understands. Goes. **COLETTE** looks to **DANNO**. She squeezes his shoulder on the way out, a show of support, follows after **RENE**. **DANNO** looks after them. He wants to go after them, to follow **RENE**. He starts, takes a few steps towards them. But stops. After what feels like forever for him but is most likely for us is a small amount of time, **DANNO** chooses. Walks off in the completely opposite direction of either of them. Alone. Music up as he goes.)*

(blackout)

End of Play

ABOUT THE PLAYWRIGHT

Crystal Skillman is a Brooklyn-based playwright.

Her play *Cut*, produced by The Management in Spring 2011 earned a critic's pick in a rave from *The New York Times*. *Cut* is scheduled to open in Boston at Apollinaire Theatre Company this spring.

Other recent productions also include: *The Vigil Or The Guided Cradle* (Impetuous Theater Group/Theater; 2010 New York Innovative Theatre Award for Outstanding Full Length Script); *Nobody* and *Birthday* (Rising Phoenix Rep in New York, Side Project in Chicago, U.K. premiere in 2010 at Waterloo East, Camden Fringe 2011 with Kibo Productions); *Action Philosophers!* (stage adaptation from the graphic novel, which premiered in the Comic Book Theater Festival, at the Brick Theatre, Summer 2011).

Upcoming plays include: *Sex And Death In London, Another Kind Of Love,* and *Wild* (debuting in Chicago with Kid Brooklyn Productions under the direction of Evan Caccippoli) as well as her new play commission for Vampire Cowboys, *Geek*, will premiere in Spring 2013 in New York.

Crystal was recently named one of Manhattan "Best Ofs" for *OurTownNY* magazine, and was selected as one of NYTheatre.com's fifteen "People of the Year" for 2011. She is represented by Joseph Rosswog at The Gersh Agency and is a member of the MCC Theater Playwrights' Coalition, Rising Phoenix Rep, as well as an alumni member of the Women's Project and Soho Rep lab.

You can learn more about her at: https://profiles.google.com/crystalskillman/about

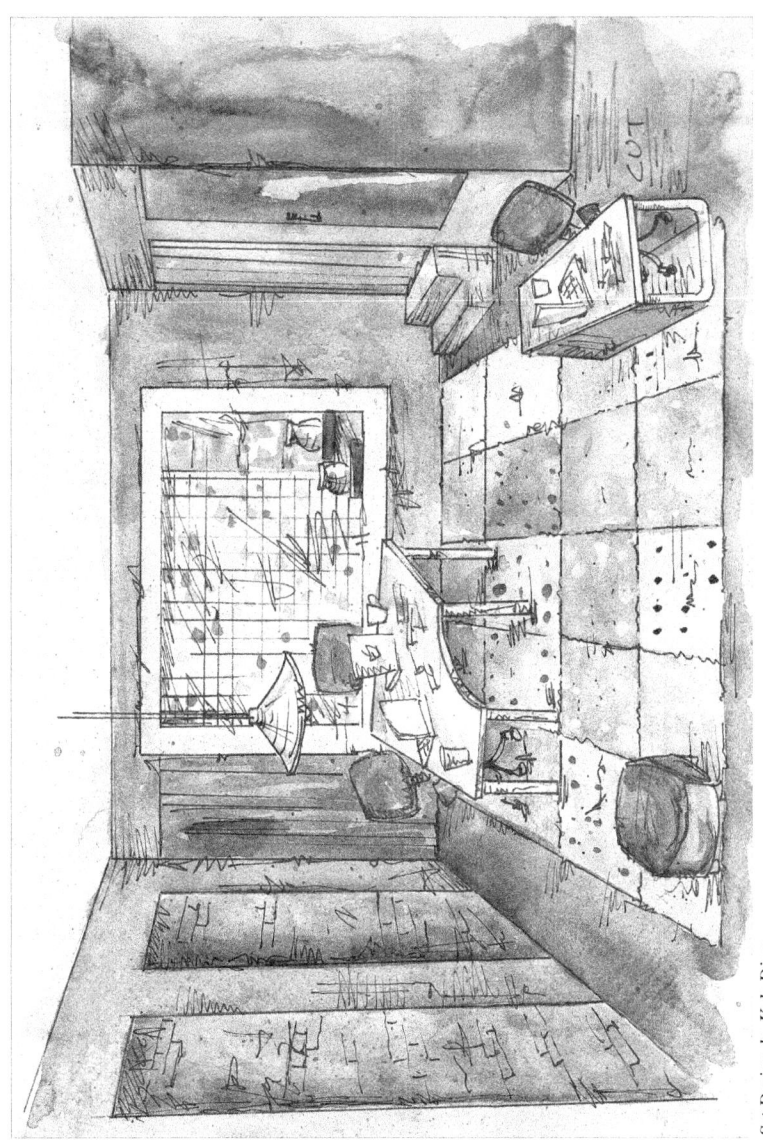

Set Design by Kyle Druom

PROP LIST

Top of Show
　Phones
　iPhone
　Bluetooth or headset for DANNO
　Computers

Scene 1
　Fish tacos
　Label, DVDs, pen [or computer]
　Framed photo of husband
　Pink cue cards

Scene 3
　Nookbook
　Old nookbook
　Business card
　Blue teddy bear with chocolate

Scene 4
　Bluetooth

Scene 6
　Top of scene – Drinks

Scene 7
　Disk with Jessica footage

Scene 8
　Top of scene – Drinks, beer for DANNO
　Yodel cake with candle
　Blue teddy bear, from SCENE 3

Scene 9
　Package
　Various destroyable office items
　Disk

Scene 11
　Top of scene – Drinks, cake, bear from SCENE 8
　NYU t-shirt, costume

Scene 12
　Package, bottle, pills

Scene 13
　Top of scene – Keys to Danno's car

See what people are saying about
CUT...

"For decades Hollywood's sick soul has provided cannon fodder for novelists and screenwriters. With *Cut*...playwright Crystal Skillman presents a modest "Hurlyburly" for our time, taking aim at reality television...the real star is the script, bristling with vitality in a compact 90 minutes."
– Andy Webster, *The New York Times*

"Crystal Skillman's surprisingly touching and insightful new play about three Los Angeles reality television writers explores free will in a fresh context. "It's like *Our Town* but in 'The Ladies of Malibu,' everyone's rich and we narrate their lives," one of the characters says of their series, a combination of the "Real Housewives" shows and "Jersey Shore." But when the question becomes whether the writers have the same control over their own lives, Skillman uncovers a universal issue that strikes to the core of human existence."
– Suzy Evans (Critics Pick), *Backstage*

"'I believe God is a shitty producer. He doesn't know how to cut anything right,' Colette says, toward the end of *Cut*. It may be blasphemy to say so, but if Colette has it right and God is a shitty producer, then Skillman and Sturiano(The Management) are clearly very good ones. *Cut* is a smart, crisp, and exciting piece of theatrical craft."
– Loren Noveck, *NYTheatre.com*

"There's more to find the deeper you look into *Cut*. Reality shows take a situation engineered for maximum conflict, splice it together into an even more artificially heightened plot, and add confessional monologues for an illusory documentary feel. Skillman mimics this structure: scenes jump back and forth in time, and characters justify their actions through soliloquies. But she uses these devices to complicate its characters rather than reducing them to caricatures."
– Aaron Grunfeld, *New York Theatre Review*

OTHER TITLES AVAILABLE FROM SAMUEL FRENCH

BIRTHDAY & NOBODY

Two Plays by Crystal Skillman

BIRTHDAY

Dramatic Comedy / 1m, 1f / Simple Set

In *Birthday*, an anxious young woman slips away from a unwelcoming birthday party in a bar only to discover a stranger sitting in the other room. Confiding old secrets and past mistakes as the party rages nearby, they find they may have a chance to forgive themselves and each other.

> "*Birthday* is a romantic comedy, sort of; it's a lovely, sweet play of connection and camaraderie. Skillman picks up details of the trappings of our lives and makes them sing resonantly."
> – *NYTheatre.com*

NOBODY

Drama / 2m, 4f / Simple Set

In *Nobody* six people come together, each for their own reasons, at a restaurant on the Lower East Side. Obsessively going over the events of the day, they grasp at trying to come to terms with their disjointed lives and their singular, unsettling dream.

> "Skillman has these people reveal themselves, inadvertently and almost in passing, in little breathtaking non-sequitur asides...this is all that *Nobody* is about—the ways that in fact everybody is Somebody, because of those idiosyncratic, individual details that make us so and sometimes prevent us from connecting as we intend."
> – *NYTheatre.com*

SAMUELFRENCH.COM

OTHER TITLES AVAILABLE FROM SAMUEL FRENCH

ENJOY

Toshiki Okada
English translation by Aya Ogawa

Experimental, Dark Comedy / 6m, 4f / Minimal Set

From acclaimed Japanese director/playwright Toshiki Okada, Artistic Director of the internationally-lauded chelfitsch Theatre Company, comes a chronicle of post-college ennui and 21st Century relationships in Japan's Lost Generation. The static lives of several self-obsessed GenX comic book store clerks are thrown out of balance by the presence of a younger female co-worker, who rightly makes them question the meaning of their lives in a shifting socio-economic landscape. Written in the hyper-colloquial style Okada has become famous for, this play is presented for the first time in English in a translation by Japanese American playwright Aya Ogawa, and was met with massive critical praise upon its New York premiere.

"Listless characters translate easily to a different culture, the blunt colloquial language elevates this drama into something more daring...Distinguished by a style that turns inarticulateness into the sort of poetry that rewards close listening. Mr. Okada, with the help of a very deft translation by Aya Ogawa, makes sure that even if it take a while to communicate a thought, a mood of indulgence and despair emerges clearly."
– *The New York Times*

"Toshiki Okada's new play deserves the attention of a major theatrical event. Meditations on age, failure, and finance read clearly as existentialism for the reigning recession. Like the best works of the theater of the absurd, Enjoy turns its humility into philosophy."
– *Backstage*

SAMUELFRENCH.COM

OTHER TITLES AVAILABLE FROM SAMUEL FRENCH

BE A GOOD LITTLE WIDOW

Bekah Brunstetter

Dramatic Comedy / 2m, 2f / Interior

Young wife Melody has never been to a funeral – until her husband dies in a plane crash. Expected to instantly assume proper widowhood, Melody is left to wonder, what's the right way to grieve? Fortunately, her mother-in-law is a professional. Widow, that is. Under her guidance, Melody must try her best to be a good little widow. A sad comedy about loss and longing.

> "Delicately satisfying…[Ms. Brunstetter] writes fresh, unfussy dialogue and characters who earn their laughs and emotional moments by honest means."
> – *The New York Times*

> "Bekah Brunstetter's powerful new play marries the humor and sadness of grief. Brunstetter's words pierce the soul, and she makes the depths of the human experience profoundly relatable…Her multidimensional characters' pain radiated through my veins, and at the end, I just wanted to feel it all over again. Critic's Pick."
> – *Backstage*

SAMUELFRENCH.COM

OTHER TITLES AVAILABLE FROM SAMUEL FRENCH

A SMALL FIRE

Adam Bock

Drama / 2m, 2f / Interior

Adam Bock's meticulously crafted *A Small Fire* follows John and Emily Bridges, a long-married couple whose happy, middle-class lives are upended when Emily falls victim to a mysterious disease. As her senses are slowly stripped away – smell, taste, sight – Emily resolves to remain engaged with her community, relying on John to help her run her company and experience her daughter Jenny's wedding. But her stoic outlook reaches a breaking point when the disease steals her hearing, leaving her with nothing but touch to communicate with the world. Suddenly, she is completely dependant on the husband whose endless devotions she had always taken for granted.

"The play is…raucous, funny and unexpectedly touching, as we are made intimate witnesses to a frank demonstration of how much of life, of love and of happiness remain within reach even when so much appears to be lost."
– *The New York Times*

"*A Small Fire* is a small play, tightly focused and written close to the vest, but its small virtues are numerous and meaningful; in retrospect, they begin to loom very large"
– *Village Voice*

SAMUELFRENCH.COM

www.ingramcontent.com/pod-product-compliance
Lightning Source LLC
Chambersburg PA
CBHW070649300426
44111CB00013B/2336